HOUGHTON MIFFLIN

Soar to Success

Student Guide
Level 2

Authors
David Chard
J. David Cooper

HOUGHTON MIFFLIN   BOSTON

Printed in China

ISBN-13: 978-0-618-94083-7
ISBN-10: 0-618-94083-9

123456789-SDP-13 12 11 10 09 08

HOUGHTON MIFFLIN

Soar to Success

Contents

● Name _____

Short *a*

Read the words and the sentences.
Choose a word from each box to complete each sentence.

bat   bad

1 Dad bought me a _____.

cap   cat

2 I put on a _____.

rag   ran

3 We all _____.

mat   nap

4 Dad had a _____!

Name _____

Short *a*, *i*

Put these letters together to write words that have the short *a* or short *i* sound.

  1 g + a + s = _____

 **2** b + i + b = _____

  3 b + a + g = _____

  4 s + i + x = _____

Now use the words you wrote to complete these sentences.

5 The baby has food on her _____.

6 The cat has _____ kittens.

7 Tim cannot pick up the big _____.

8 The bus needs _____ to go.

● Name _____

Question

Both stories are about cats. Draw a cat from each story. Then tell how Sam the cat is different from a wild cat.

Sam	Wild Cat

_____

_____

Name _____

Short *o*

Read the words and the sentences.
Choose a word from each box to complete each sentence.

Mom   Mop

1 _____ is in the kitchen.

pit   pot

2 She has a big _____.

cot   got

3 What has she _____ in there?

lot   lob

4 She has a _____ of jam!

● Name _____

Short *u*

Read the words and the sentences.
Choose a word from each box to complete each sentence.

dug   tug

1 Pam and I _____.

mug   mud

2 We brought _____ in the kitchen.

bus   us

3 Dad was mad at _____.

hug   hut

4 We were sad until we had a _____.

Name _____

Summarize

Which of the jobs you read about would you most like to do?
Draw yourself doing it. Write a sentence about the job you chose.

The Job for Me

_____

_____

Name _____

Short *e*

Use sounds you know to read the questions.
Circle Yes or No to answer each question.

1 Can a bus be red?   Yes   No

2 Do some men jog?   Yes   No

3 Is your bed in the mud?   Yes   No

4 Can you fly in a jet?   Yes   No

5 Can you get a surprise in a box?   Yes   No

6 Would you run on a bad leg?   Yes   No

7 Is a tub a good pet?   Yes   No

8 Does a hen eat gum?   Yes   No

Name _____

Short *a, e, i, o, u*

Listen as the following words are read: *truck, dress, desk, blocks, drum.* What is the short vowel sound in each word? Write the letter that stands for this sound on the tag for the picture of that word.

Name _____

Short *a*, *e*, *i*, *o*, *u*

● Use sounds you know to read the sentences.
Circle the letter that best completes each word.
Write the word.

(1) Ben is my special p__t. a e i o u   _____

(2) He is a big d__g.   a e i o u   _____

(3) Ben can s__t, dig, and run. a e i o u _____

(4) He likes to n__p on my bed. a e i o u _____

(5) I wash him in a t__b. a e i o u   _____

Name _____

Summarize

Which of the animals you read about was your favorite? Draw it. Write a sentence about something it does.

A Special Animal

_____

_____

Name _____

Long *a* (CVC*e*)

Read the sentences. Circle each word that has a long *a* sound.

1 Poor Jane!

2 Her mom made her a big cake.

3 But the cake had a sad fate.

4 Jane could not save it.

5 She gave it to her dog Jake.

6 Jake ate the cake.

Name _____

Long *a* (CVC*e*)

Read each sentence. Use the letters in the box to complete the words.

1 | m n | My _____a_____e is Nate.

2 | c f | I have a big _____a_____e.

3 | n m | I have a long _____a_____e.

4 | t m | But I am very _____a_____e.

5 | c g | This is my _____a_____e.

6 | s l | It is for _____a_____e!

Name _____

Long *a* (CVC*e*)

Read the sentences. Draw a line to match each one with a picture.

1 Dane and Zane are both the same.

2 Dale came in the gate.

3 Gabe was too late to win the race.

4 Let us go to the cave by the lake.

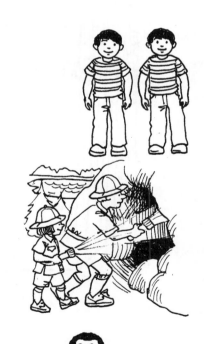

Name _____

Question

Both stories are about things you could find in a store. Think of something you could find in a store that you would like to give to a special friend. Draw it in the box. Write your friend's name on the tag. Label the gift below.

Name _____

Long Vowels *a* CVC*e a, i*

Put these letters together to write words. Some words will have a short *a* or a short *i* sound. Some will have a long *a* or a long *i* sound.

1 k + i + t + e = _____

2 k + i + t = _____

3 s + l + i + d = _____

4 s + l + i + d + e = _____

5 t + a + p + e = _____

6 t + a + p = _____

7 m + a + d = _____

8 m + a + d + e = _____

9 c + a + n = _____

10 c + a + n + e = _____

11 P + e + t + t + e = _____

12 p + e + t = _____

Now write the words under the correct vowel sound.

Short Vowel Sound	Long Vowel Sound

Name _____

Long a, i (CVCe) *a*, *i*

Read the sentences and letters. Draw a line to match each sentence to the letter that completes the incomplete word. Write the missing letters in the words.

1 We had a _____ice time at the lake.

2 Dave has two pet _____ice.

3 Be on time. Do not be _____ate.

4 Mike put on a _____ape and a hat.

5 You can fix that rip with _____ape.

6 Do you like to ride your _____ike?

| c |
| l |
| t |
| n |
| b |
| m |

Name _____

Long a, i (CVCe *a*, *i*)

Read the sentences. Draw a line to match each one with a picture.

1 We like to hike by the lake.

2 We can dive into the waves.

3 We can race on bikes.

4 It is nice here by the fire.

Name _____

Summarize

Draw a picture of you and a friend doing something together. Then write a sentence about friends.

Name _____

Long *o* (CVC*e*)

Read the story. Number the pictures in order.

I wake up, and I see a beautiful rose.

I poke the rose. Water comes out!

I look at the rose. It is on a hose.

What a good joke!

_____

_____

_____

_____

Level 2, Book 6, *Outside* **23**

Name _____

Long *u* (CVC*e*)

Use the sounds you know to read this story. Circle the words with a long u sound. Write them below.

I see a huge mule. It is cute.

I sing it a quiet tune. I even play the lute.

The mule runs away. How rude!

_____

_____

_____

_____

_____

● Name _____

Question

Both stories talk about beautiful things. What thing in the stories do you think is most beautiful? Draw it. Write why you think it is beautiful.

Name _____

Long CVC*e*

Draw a line from each child to the picture of what he or she needs.

Name _____

Long CVCe

Circle the word in finish each sentence. Write the word on the line. Then circle all the words in the sentences with long vowel sounds.

1 _____ is a fun time of year.

cute   June

2 I like to _____ into the lake.

dive   rude

3 I can eat a huge _____ of ice.

cone   home]

4 I can ride my bike _____ and there.

note   here

5 I can even run a _____!

hole   race

Name _____

Long CVC*e*

Read the story. Circle each word with a long vowel sound.

Mose is too busy to get his cake.

Pete rides his bike here to get it.

Pete takes the huge cake home.

Can Pete see with the cake in his face?

No! He rides into the lake.

Mose saves Pete with a rope. He also saves his cake.

Now write each circled word under the long vowel sound it has.

long *a*	long *e*	long *i*	long *o*	long *u*

Name _____

Question

Both stories are about bikes. What do Pete and Zeke do to have a safe ride on their bikes? Draw them on their bikes. Write a sentence to explain how they have a safe ride.

_____

_____

_____

Name _____

Two Sounds for *g*

Read these sentences. Circle Yes or No to answer whether each is true or not. Then circle each word that has the same sound for *g* as *gum*. Underline each word that has the same sound for *g* as *gem*.

Is this true?

1 You can open a gate.   Yes   No

2 Some kids like to dig big holes.   Yes   No

3 All bugs are huge.   Yes   No

4 It is important to eat mugs.   Yes   No

5 A bird cage can hop.   Yes   No

6 A book page can be made of gas.   Yes   No

Name _____

Two Sounds for *c*

Read the words and the sentences. Write a word from the box to complete each sentence. Then circle each word that has the same sound for *c* as *cob*. Underline each word that has the same sound for *c* as *lace*.

face	car	ice	race

1 Cal can run a good _____ .

2 Ace has a big _____ .

3 This _____ is very cold!

4 Cam has a cut on his _____ .

Name _____

Summarize

Both stories talk about ways to take care of a pet dog. What do you think is the most important part of taking care of a pet dog? Draw a picture of how you would help. Write your answer in a sentence.

_____

_____

_____

Name _____

Consonant Clusters with *r*

Read the sentences. Draw a line to match each one with aa picture.

1 Can Frog cram it all in?

2 The crate is full to the brim!

3 Frog trips and drops the crate.

4 Frog gripes about the grime.

5 Crab can drag the crate for Frog!

Name _____

Consonant Clusters with *s, l*

Read the story. Circle each word with a cluster with *s*.
Underline each word with a cluster with *l*.

Glen likes to race on skates.

He is fast when he glides on his blades.

Then he stubs the tip of his skate.

He flops flat on his face!

Glen gasps. He is in last place.

Glen must do his best now.

He skates past the other kids and wins.

Now he can rest!

● Name _____

Question

Both stories are about animal tracks. Draw and label three of the animals that made tracks.

Name _____

Double Final Consonants

What a mess!

Circle the words with double final consonants. Write the words you circled.

_____   _____

_____   _____

_____   _____

_____   _____

Name _____

VCCV Pattern

Read the sentences. Draw a line to match each one to a picture.

1 Who will help me sew a napkin?

2 Who will help me find my mittens?

3 Who will help me make a puppet?

4 Who will help me fix my rocket?

5 Who will help me fill a basket?

Name _____

Summarize

Both stories are about games kids can play. Draw a picture of a game you can play when it is nice. Then draw a picture of a game you can play when it rains. Write a sentence telling about each game.

Name _____

Digraph *sh*

Read the words and the sentences. Write a word from the box to complete each sentence.

| smash   shut   trash   rush   ship   shop |

1 She bought a fish at the pet _____.

2 If you drop the dish, it will _____.

3 He ran past me in a huge _____.

4 We will cross the water on a _____.

5 It is cold in here. _____ the door!

6 Put that junk in the _____ can.

Name _____

Digraph *ch*

Read the story. Circle the words with the *ch* sound at the beginning. Underline the words with the *ch* sound at the end.

Chip asks Rich to come over for lunch.

Chip goes to his kitchen.

He bakes a chicken.

Chip tastes the chicken.

Crunch. Crunch. Crunch.

Chip sets a bunch of grapes on the table.

He tastes the grapes.

Munch. Munch. Munch.

Too bad! Chip ate too much.

Now Chip and Rich must just sit and chat!

● Name _____

Question

Both stories tell about animals. Which of these animals would you most like to see? Draw a picture of it. Write a sentence or two to explain why you would like to see this animal.

_____

_____

_____

Name _____

Digraphs *th* and *tch*

Read the sentences. Underline the words that have the *th* sound. Circle the words that have the *tch* sound.

1 My dog can catch and fetch a bone.

2 I fell on the path with a thud.

3 She bakes a batch of muffins.

4 I have an itch to scratch on my back.

5 Latch the door during your bath.

6 Did you snatch that sketch?

Name _____

Digraph *wh*

Read the words and the sentences. Write a word from the box to complete each sentence.

Which	when	why	while	Where

1 I go to bed _____ I want to rest.

2 Do you know _____ that whale is white?

3 _____ wig will match this dress best?

4 _____ did you hide the eggs?

5 I will sing _____ you do a jig.

Name _____

Summarize

Both stories are about things chicks do. Draw a comic strip showing a day in the life of a chick. Write a sentence about each picture you draw.

_____
_____

_____

● Name _____

Vowel Pairs *ai*, *ay*

Read the story. Circle the words with the vowel pair *ai*.
Underline the words with the vowel pair *ay*.

Gail and Fay plan a trip to the bay.

They pack a spade and a pail.

They want to sail and play!

Gail and Fay take the train.

They walk down a trail.

It is not the right way to go.

Then the sky turns gray and it rains.

They stay in a shop. They wait for the rain to stop.

This was not a good day to go to the bay!

Name _____

Compound Words

Look at the pictures. Read the words in the box. Figure out which compound word each set of pictures shows. Write that word in the space to the right.

dishcloth	sidewalk	flagpole	pancake

1 ☐ + ☐ = _____

2 ☐ + ☐ = _____

3 ☐ + ☐ = _____

4 ☐ + ☐ = _____

● Name _____

Question

Both stories talk about things you will need for outdoor activities such as hiking or camping. Draw and label three things you would need to go hiking or camping. Write a sentence explaining how you would use the things you drew.

_____

_____

_____

Name _____

Vowel Pairs *ow*, *ou*

Read both words. Pick the one with the /ou/ sound. Write it to complete the sentence.

town **track**

My house is on the west side of the _____.

mutt **mouse**

Scout pets the brown _____ on its snout.

clown **clam**

The sad _____ made me frown.

sprout **smell**

The flower will not _____ without water from the spout.

Name _____

Suffixes *-ly*, *-ful*

Circle the word to finish each sentence. Write the word on the line.

(1) I believe our dog is the most _____ dog ever.

playful   openly

(2) Cliff is a very _____ boy.

sadly   friendly

(3) After they won the game, the kids were _____.

wishful   joyful

(4) Miss Brown is so nice that she gives help _____.

gladly   safely

(5) May is _____ with people she does not know.

bashful   tuneful

(6) I am _____ that I did well on the math test.

hopeful   stressful

Name _____

Question

Both stories tell about special work clothes that people wear to do their jobs. Draw a picture of someone you can think of that wears special work clothes. Write a riddle or some clues to help others guess what your picture shows.

_____

_____

_____

_____

Name _____

Vowel Pairs *ee*, *ea*

**Read the letter. Circle the words with the
vowel pairs *ee* and *ea*.**

Dear Neal,

It is fun to stay at the beach.

We can swim in the sea and sleep under the sun.

For a treat, we eat peach ice cream. It is sweet!

We will leave in a week. I will see you soon!

Your friend,

Jean

Write each circled word under the word with the same vowel pair.

greet	flea

Name _____

The Endings *-tion* and *-ture* in Two-Syllable Words

Read the sentences. Circle the words that end with *-tion*. Underline the words that end with *-ture*.

Bea goes on vacation.

She wants to see the most joyful bird in the nation.

It is so happy. No one wants to capture it.

Bea looks in the pasture and up the steep hill.

Bea sees the creature in a tree.

Every action it takes is graceful.

Every motion it makes is beautiful.

Bea wants to take its picture!

Write each circled or underline word under the word with the same ending.

station	fixture

Name _____

Summarize

Both stories are about ice cream. Pick one of the strange ice cream flavors from "Sweet Miss Kate" and draw a picture to show how that flavor could be made. Then write a sentence or two explaining how the ice cream could get to the store after it was made.

My Ice Cream

_____

_____

_____

Name _____

r-Controlled Vowels -ar

Read the words and the sentences. Write a word from the box to complete each sentence.

jar	car	yarn	park	farm	bark

1 I made a hat with _____.

2 My _____ can go fast.

3 You can see a pig on a _____.

4 Listen to the dog _____.

5 We will eat jam from this _____.

6 Meet me by the slide at the _____.

Name _____

r-Controlled Vowels -or, -ore

Read the story. Circle all the words with the /ôr/ sound.

Mom and I bought corn and pork at the store.

Dad told us, "I wish to eat on the porch."

I brought a seat for him. Mom brought him a plate on a tray.

Dad said, "I need a fork, too!"

As Dad ate, there was a storm. The rain made Dad wet. When he got up, he slid and fell on his tray.

Dad was sad. His pants tore and he was sore. I was sad, too. It was my chore to sweep up the floor!

Write circled words spelled with *or* in the left column and circled words spelled with *ore* in the right column.

or Words	*ore* Words

Name _____

Question

Both stories are about parks. What kind of park do you like to visit? What do you like to do at the park? Draw where you like to go and what you like to do. Write a sentence or two about what you do.

Name _____

r-Controlled Vowels -ir, -ur, -er

Read the words and the sentences. Write a word from the box to complete each sentence.

Squirt	fern	first	burn	sternly	turn

1 It is Lee's _____ to go down the slide.

2 These sticks will _____ well in the fire.

3 I told my dog _____ not to eat my socks.

4 Brad picks a _____ in the forest.

5 Clay ran so fast he came in _____ place.

6 _____ some lotion on your sunburn.

Name _____

r-Controlled Vowels

Read the sentences. Draw a line to match each one with a picture.

1 It is hard to eat corn on the cob with a fork.

2 Jordan fell in the dirt.

3 The store is far away, so we will take my car.

4 Tell the nurse if you need her help.

58 Level 2, Book 17, *School Days*

Name _____

r-Controlled Vowels

Read the story. Circle the words in the story
that have the /är/ sound, the /ôr/ sound,
or the /ûr/ sound.

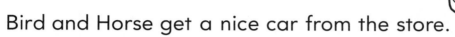

Bird and Horse get a nice car from the store.
First, Bird drives.
Bird takes her time. She does not go fast or far.
She does not want to hurt the car.
Horse has to wait and wait for her turn. What a bore!
Now Horse drives.
The street curves, so Horse must swerve.
Smash! Horse is glad she did not hurt the car! .
Now Horse can drive some more!

**Write each circled word under the word or words with the
same sound.**

park	torn/tore	fern/girl/fur

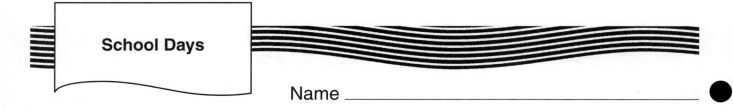

Name _____

Summarize

Both stories are about things children do at school. Draw a picture of something you like to do at school and write a sentence to describe your picture.

[blank drawing box]

_____

_____

_____

● Name _____

Vowel Pairs *oa*, *ow*

● Use sounds you know to read the story. Then find all the words with the long *o* sound in the story. Write them on the lines.

A toad and a crow had a contest. The goal was to show who could make a plant grow faster. The crow put his plant in the sun and gave it water. The toad yelled at his plant, "Grow, grow!" The crow's plant grew. The toad just got a sore throat from yelling.

Name _____

Endings *-er*, *-est*

Put the word and the ending in the box together to make a new word. Write the word to complete the sentence. Read the completed sentence.

1 | tall est | Which tree is the _____?

2 | long er | This street is _____ than that one.

3 | sick er | Fred feels _____ than Marge does.

4 | small est | That is the _____ fish I have ever seen!

Summarize

Both stories are about birds. Draw a picture of a bird from one of the stories that you would like to see in real life. Write one thing you learned from the stories about this bird.

_____

_____

_____

Name _____

Base Words and Endings: *-es*, *-ies*

Read the sentences. Add *-es* or *-ies* to the word below each sentence, and write the new word to complete the sentence.

1 My _____ like to fetch bones.

(puppy)

2 I saw three _____ at the park today.

(baby)

3 If I drop this tray, the _____ will break.

(glass)

4 Do you see those white _____ of light?

(flash)

5 On Sunday I take two _____.

(class)

6 Help me swat these _____!

(fly)

Name _____

Base Words and Endings: *-s*, *-es*, *-ies*

Read the word on each truck. Add *-s*, *-es*, or *-ies* to the word and write the new word you make in the correct column of the chart.

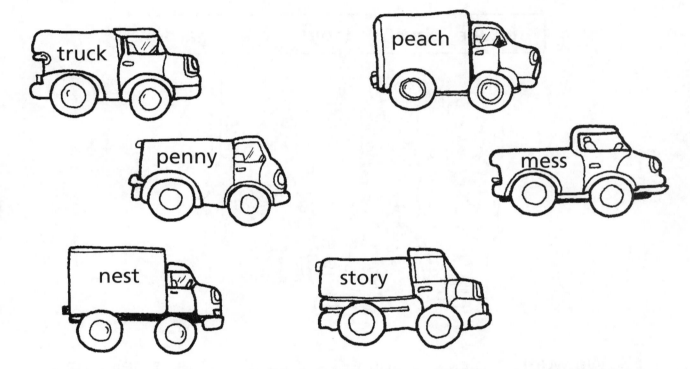

-s words	-es words	-ies words

Name _____

Base Words and Endings: -s, -es, -ies

Read the words and the sentences. Pick words from the box and add -s, -es, or -ies. Write the new words to complete the sentences.

| flower | bush | lady | tree | garden |

1 We want to pick out some _____ that smell nice.

2 These _____ will help us.

3 Many people shop for stuff for their _____.

4 Do you have any tall fir _____?

5 We could get some rose _____ for our backyard.

● Name _____

Question

Both stories are about puppies. Draw a picture of a puppy you would like to take care of. Write a list of rules for taking care of this puppy.

① _____

② _____

③ _____

Name _____

Words with *nd*, *nt*, *mp*

Read the words and the sentences. Write a word from the box to complete each sentence.

stamp	sand	went	bent	limp	stand

(1) During the storm all the lights _____ out.

(2) We cannot play tennis because our net is _____.

(3) We must _____ in a long line for tickets.

(4) Put a _____ on the letter before you mail it.

(5) I like to dig holes in the _____ at the beach.

(6) The dog with a hurt leg walks with a _____.

Name _____

Words with *ng*, *nk*

Circle the word to finish each sentence. Write the word on the line.

1 There is a pretty gem in that _____.

rink   ring

2 Her hurt arm is in a _____.

slink   sling

3 He _____ the picture on a nail.

hunk   hung

4 The bird flaps its _____.

wings   winks

5 A bee _____ my hand.

stung   stunk

Name _____

Question

Both stories are about George Washington. Draw something important that happened to George Washington. Write a sentence to explain your drawing.

_____

_____

_____

Name _____

The *-er* Ending in Two-Syllable Words

The storm started at dinner time. Thunder boomed and boomed. Our dog hid under the bed. Mom said we had better close all the windows. She did not want to get rain on the rugs. After we ate, we put on our robes and slippers and watched the rain.

Name _____

The *-er* Ending in Two-Syllable Words

Read the words and the sentences. Write a word from the box to complete each sentence.

| father | better | winner | blender | summer | winter |

1 The big race will take place on a hot _____ day.

2 My _____ and uncle will run in the race.

3 The _____ will get a nice prize.

4 My uncle is a _____ runner than my dad.

5 He runs all year long, even through the snow in _____.

6 After the race we will mix up a snack in the _____!

Name _____

The *-er* Ending in Two-Syllable Words

Read the sentences. Draw a line to match each one with a picture.

(1) We hung a big banner on the wall.

(2) He hurt his finger in the door.

(3) I bought these peaches from a farmer.

(4) We will vote to pick a leader.

(5) The pitcher throws the ball to the batter.

Name _____

Question

Both stories tell about things you could be when you grow up. Draw a picture of what you want to be when you grow up. Write a sentence to explain why you want to do that job.

_____

_____

_____

Name _____

The Long *e* Sound for *y*

Read the sentences. Draw a line to match each one with a picture.

1 It was a windy day.

2 Jan plants a cherry tree.

3 I can carry those plates.

4 Peggy tells us funny jokes.

5 The kitty jumps up on the bed.

Name _____

The Long *e* Sound for *y*

Read the story.

Jerry saw a creepy show with his buddy Benny.

Now Jerry thinks he sees creepy, hairy beasts everywhere.

"Do not be silly," said Benny. "There are no creepy, hairy beasts here."

"Still, I think I will go to funny shows from now on!" said Jerry.

Write the words that end with a *y* with the long *e* sound.

_____   _____

_____   _____

_____   _____

_____   _____

Name _____

The Long *e* Sound for *y*

Read the story. Circle the words that end with a *y* that has the long *e* sound.

Cindy needs her fairy godmother.

She does not want to be late for the party!

Her clothes are dirty and dusty.

The fairy gives her a clean dress.

Her hair is frizzy.

The fairy makes her hair curly.

Now Cindy is as pretty as a daisy!

Name _____

Question

Both stories are about different kinds of weather. Draw a picture of the kind of weather you like best and what you like to do in this kind of weather. Write a sentence or two to explain why you like this kind of weather best.

_____

_____

_____

Name _____

The *-le* Ending in Two-Syllable Words

Read the sentences. Write a word from the box in each sentence.

mumble	candle	giggle	puddle	apple	puzzle

1 Blow out the _____.

2 She'll _____ when she hears the joke.

3 The rain left a big _____ on the street.

4 We're trying to solve the _____.

5 I can't hear you when you _____.

6 The _____ is red and juicy.

Name _____

The Prefix *un-*

Circle the word to finish each sentence. Write the word on the line.

1 The stacks of books are _____.

unable   uneven

2 An icy road can be _____.

unsafe   unsaid

3 Our team is _____!

unlike   unbeaten

4 I like _____ carrots.

unhooked   uncooked

5 He looked for an _____ pencil.

unreal   unbroken

Draw an unhappy face in the box.

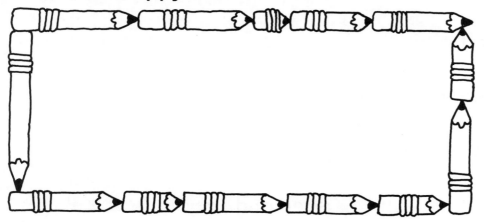

● Name _____

Summarize

Both stories are about people in families and how they are alike or different from each other. Draw a picture of yourself and someone else in your family. Write a sentence telling how you are the same. Write a sentence telling how you are different.

Alike: _____

_____

Different: _____

_____

Name _____

Contractions

Read both words. Turn them into a contraction. Write the contraction to complete the sentence.

1 | Do not | _____ drop the rocks!

2 | He will | _____ do his homework before dinner.

3 | She is | _____ my best friend.

4 | We are | _____ afraid of the dark.

Name _____

Contractions

Read the sentences. Draw a line to match each one with a picture.

(1) Let's bake a big cake.

(2) I'm late for class!

(3) That's the shirt I want.

(4) You're taller than my sister.

(5) We'll ride our bikes to the park.

Name _____

Contractions

Read the words and the sentences. Write the contraction from the box that best completes each sentence.

don't	They've	can't	It's	I'll	She's

1 _____ lift those chairs for you.

2 I _____ know where I left my backpack.

3 Mike _____ go to the play with us.

4 _____ very sleepy by her bedtime.

5 _____ found a house that they like.

6 _____ hard to sneak up on a cat.

Name _____

Summarize

Both stories are about taking a plane trip. Draw a comic strip about taking a plane trip somewhere. Draw one part of the trip in each panel. Write captions to explain what is going on in each scene.

Name _____

Silent Consonants *gh*, *k* in *kn*, and *b* in *mb*

Read the sentences. Draw a line to match each sentence with a picture.

1 The kitten climbs the ladder.

2 He slipped and hurt his knee.

3 Mom is cutting with a small knife.

4 She taught her dog a trick.

5 There is a big knot in the rope.

● Name _____

Silent Consonants *gh*, *k* in *kn*, and *b* in *mb*

Circle the word with the silent consonant to finish each sentence. Write the word on the line.

1 During its _____, Penny's nice kite got stuck in a tree.
fling flight

2 It's on that _____.
leaf limb

3 Penny can't _____ up to get it.
climb carry

4 She doesn't _____ where the ladder is.
know no

5 Look! A chipmunk will _____ the kite out of the tree!
sock knock

Name _____

Silent Consonants *gh*, *k* in *kn*, and *b* in *mb*

Read the sentences. Circle the words that start with a silent consonant. Underline the words that end with a silent consonant.

1 Jake cut the loaf with a knife.

2 The sailor twists the rope into a knot.

3 That brown comb looks nice in your hair.

4 Even though I was careful, I still fell.

5 Sam knows many songs.

Name _____

Summarize

Both stories are about fun outdoor activities. Draw a picture of yourself doing your favorite outdoor activity. Write a sentence about why you like to do this activity.

_____

_____

Name _____

Vowel Pairs *oo, ew*

Read the riddles. Answer each one with a word from the box.

pool	newspaper	boot	stew

1 I'm a tasty food. Eat me with a fork or spoon. What am I?

_____

2 I'm something you can read. I'm not a book. What am I?

_____

3 I'm something to put on a foot. I'm not a sock or a slipper. What am I?

_____

4 I'm something you can swim in. I'm not a lake or a pond. What am I?

_____

Name _____

Vowel Pairs *oo, ew, ue, ou*

Read the words and the sentences. Write a word from the box to complete each sentence.

screws	blue	soon	through	room	drew

1 Matthew will _____ move to a new house.

2 He has a plan for how his new _____ will look.

3 He will paint the walls a light _____.

4 He will put up all the pictures he _____, too.

5 He knows how to hang them with nails and _____.

6 His room will look nice when he's _____.

Name _____

Vowel Pairs *oo*, *ew*, *ue*, *ou*

pool	trout
few	blue
threw	food
group	glue
book	wood

Read the words on the bowl of soup and circle all the ones with the sound of /ōō/. Write each circled word in the correct box below.

oo	ew	ue	ou
_____	_____	_____	_____
_____	_____	_____	_____

●Name _____

Question

In both stories, a butterfly hatches. Draw five steps an egg goes through to turn into a butterfly. Write a sentence about each step.

Name _____

Long *i (igh)*

| frightening | high | fight | light | tight | night |

Read the words in the box and the numbered clues. Write the word from the box that goes with each clue.

(1) not low, but _____

(2) a lamp gives _____

(3) not loose, but _____

(4) people at war do this _____

(5) something scary is _____

(6) not day, but _____

Write clues that would help someone guess the word *bright*.

_____

_____

Name _____

Long *i* (*igh*, *ie*)

Read the story. Circle the words with the long *i* sound spelled with *igh* or *ie*.

Izzy sighs loudly. She wants badly to bake a pie. Her mother might help, but she isn't home. Then her father tells her he will help. Izzy smiles brightly.

Izzy and Dad work together. He gets the pan down from a high shelf. She kneads the dough with her right hand. They work until the moon comes out and it is night.

Izzy spills flour on her thigh. Dad smears butter on his tie. Then Mom comes home and sees the kitchen. Everything is so messy that she gets a fright! But they are all happy when the pie is done. It is a beautiful sight.

Name _____

Long *i* (*igh*, *ie*)

This is Mud Pie City. Find the sights listed in the box on the map. Write each name next to the correct number to label that sight. Then circle words that have the long *i* sound spelled *igh* or *ie*.

1 _____

2 _____

3 _____

4 _____

5 _____

Name _____

Summarize

Draw a picture of someone using light to see something better. Write a sentence to explain your picture.

_____

_____

_____

Name _____

Base Words and Endings *-ed*, *-ing*

Circle the word to finish each sentence. Write the word on the line.

1 Mister Meers is _____ the ladder to the roof.

(climbing, climbed)

2 Last year, Mister Meers _____ two big holes in the roof.

(fixing, fixed)

3 Now, the holes need _____ again.

(fixing, fixed)

4 The roof is _____ badly.

(leaking, leaked)

5 Three inches of water have _____ into his house!

(raining, rained)

Name _____

Base Words and Endings *-ed*, *-ing*

Read the words and the sentences. Write a word from the box to complete each sentence.

rubbed	swimming	napped	sipped	digging	clapped

1 Dave went _____ in the sea this morning.

2 He felt proud because people _____ at his speed.

3 After that, he _____ some suntan lotion on his back.

4 Then he lay down and _____ on his towel.

5 When he woke up, he tried _____ in the sand to make a fort.

6 Then he _____ a cold drink to cool down.

Name _____

Question

Both stories are about animals that live in a forest. Make a guide to animal life. Draw and label three animals you could see in a forest. Then write a fact about each animal.

_____

_____

_____

_____

_____

_____

Name _____

Base Words and Endings *-ed*, *-ing*

Read the sentences. Draw a line to match each one with a picture.

1 The dog is shaking to dry off.

2 The runner raced to the finish line.

3 She is placing a book on the shelf.

4 They are hiking on the trail.

5 She smiled when she got the prize.

Name _____

Base Words and Endings *-ed*, *-ing*

Read the sentences. Draw a line to match each one with a picture.

1 The baby was hiding in the box.

2 Prue and Gus moved the chairs around.

3 We went dancing with Willy today.

4 Tammy and Tommy will go running after lunch.

5 Jean wanted to get a new car.

Name _____

Base Words and Endings *-ed*, *-ing*

Circle the word to finish each sentence. Write the word on the line.

1 Kate is _____ a scarf.

knitting quitting

2 Vince _____ his homework.

stated started

3 That dog is _____ all the bubbles!

popping painting

4 She _____ me the right way to go.

shoved showed

5 Turn off the tap and stop _____ water.

wasting washing

Name _____

Question

Both stories are about the beach. Draw something you would like to do at the beach. Write a sentence or two to describe your picture.

_____

_____

_____

Name _____

VCCV, VCV Patterns

Read the sentences. Draw a line to match each sentence with the correct picture.

(1) Dot put on goggles before she rode her motorbike.

(2) The red traffic signal told us to stop.

(3) The old hotel room used candles instead of light bulbs.

(4) We made pancakes and bacon on the hot griddle.

(5) There's a spider on the handle of my bag!

VCCV, VCV Patterns

Read the story and the words in the mixing bowl. Write only words with the VCCV pattern to complete the baker's list.

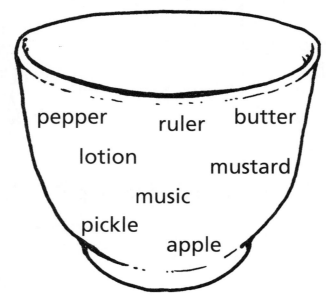

pepper   ruler   butter
lotion   mustard
music
pickle
apple

The silly baker begins to make muffins. He puts the batter in his blender. It mixes with a splatter. Then, he tastes it with his finger. He thinks it could be better. What could he add to give it more flavor?

Add these to your batter, Baker!

The
Baker's
List
_____
_____
_____
_____
_____

Name _____

VCCV, VCV Patterns

Each word names a thing. Write the word from the box that goes with that thing.

table	garden	picnic	baby

1 _____ cradle

2 _____ basket

3 _____ gate

4 _____ napkin

Name _____

Summarize

Each story talks about a way that best friends can stay in touch from far away. Draw a picture of each way. Write a sentence to describe each one.

_____

_____

_____

_____